# PASTRIES
# & BAKING

Delicious teatime treats, from classic
breads to fancy pastries

# CONTENTS

## Guide to symbols

The recipes in this book are accompanied by symbols that alert you to important information.

 Tells you how many people the recipe serves, or how much is produced.

 Indicates how much time you will need to prepare and cook a dish. Next to this symbol you will also find out if additional time is required for such things as marinating, standing, proving, or cooling. You need to read the recipe to find out exactly how much extra time is needed.

 Alerts you to what has to be done before you can begin to cook the recipe, or to parts of the recipe that take a long time to complete.

 Denotes that special equipment is required. Where possible, alternatives are given.

 Accompanies freezing information.

# Techniques

## Mix and knead yeast dough
Dough should be well combined and kneaded to a silken and elastic finish.

**1** Place the dry ingredients in a large bowl and gradually add the liquid ingredients. Combine using your fingers, digging into the bottom of the bowl and pressing the dough through your fingers to mix.

**2** When the liquid is fully incorporated, the dough should be soft but not sticky. When ready to knead, turn the dough out on to a floured surface and, with oiled fingers, fold it in half towards you.

**3** Using the heel of your hand, gently but firmly press down and away through the centre to stretch and knead the dough. Lift and rotate the dough a quarter turn.

**4** Repeat the folding, pressing and rotating 10–12 times. Let the dough rest, as directed in your recipe, then continue kneading. Each kneading will require less oil and produce a more elastic dough.

# Make brioche dough

This dough is very sticky so it is easier to make using an electric mixer. See p12 for ingredient quantities.

**1** Pour the dry ingredients into the bowl of the mixer. Using the dough hook attachment, mix on medium speed and add the milk and eggs a little at a time. Mix until smooth and fully incorporated.

**2** Once the dough is mixed and begins to come away from the edges of the bowl, add butter (at room temperature and cut into pieces). Mix again until the dough comes away from the edges.

**3** When the dough is mixed, transfer it to another large bowl. Cover with cling film and leave it to sit at room temperature for 2–3 hours, or until it doubles in size. The risen dough will be very sticky.

**4** Lightly flour a work surface and punch down the dough with your fist to deflate it. Return it to the bowl, cover with cling film, and chill to let it rise for 1¼ hours. Deflate once more, then shape and bake.

# Make pastry

Once rested, pastry dough can be used at once or stored for up to two days in a refrigerator, wrapped in cling film. This recipes makes 1kg (2¼lb) of pastry.

1 Mix 375g (13 oz) unsalted, softened butter, with 1 egg yolk and 1½ teaspoons of salt. In another bowl, mix 2 teaspoons of sugar with 100ml (3½fl oz) milk, then gradually stir it into the butter mixture.

2 Sift 500g (1lb 2oz) of plain flour into a bowl, then gradually stir it into the butter. When all the flour is added, continue mixing with a wooden spoon or gently combine with your hands.

3 Dust a work surface with flour and turn out the pastry. Using the palm of your hand, lightly knead the pastry until it forms a soft, moist dough.

4 Shape the dough into a ball, wrap it in cling film, and refrigerate for at least 2 hours. Allowing the gluten and flour to relax during chilling will prevent the dough from shrinking when in the hot oven.

# Bake pastry blind

A pastry case for a tart or pie must be pre-cooked if its filling will not be baked or baked only for a short time.

1 Once the pastry is fitted in the tin, prick the bottom with a fork. This will allow trapped air to escape during baking.

2 Cut out a circle of baking parchment, just slightly larger than the tin. Fold the parchment in half 3 times to make a triangular shape and clip the edges at regular intervals with scissors.

3 Place the parchment circle into the tin and fill it with an even layer of ceramic or metal baking beans. Bake at 180°C (350°F/ Gas 4) for 15–20 minutes – it will be partially baked.

4 When cool enough to handle, remove the beans and parchment. For fully baked pastry, return the pastry to the oven for a further 5–8 minutes, or until golden.

# Walnut bread

In France, this savoury bread is a traditional accompaniment to the cheese course.

## INGREDIENTS

350g (12 oz) strong wholemeal flour
200g (7 oz) strong white flour, plus extra
  for dusting
7g sachet easy-blend dried yeast
1½ tsp salt
1 tsp sugar
1 tbsp walnut oil, plus extra for brushing
150g (5½ oz) walnuts, coarsely chopped

## METHOD

1  Mix the first 5 ingredients in a large bowl, making a well in the centre. Stir 350ml (12fl oz) tepid water and the walnut oil into the well. Gradually add up to 100ml (3½fl oz) more water until the flour is incorporated and the dough is soft.

2  Turn out the dough on to a lightly floured surface and knead for 5–8 minutes, or until smooth and elastic. Shape into a ball.

3  Rub the inside of a dry bowl with oil. Put the dough in the bowl, cover with cling film, and leave in a warm place until doubled in size. Meanwhile, lightly dust a large baking tray with flour.

4  Punch down the dough, turn it out on to a floured surface, and knead for 1 minute. Pat the dough into a rectangle and sprinkle with the walnuts. Knead for a few more minutes, or until the nuts are evenly distributed.

5  Cut the dough in half and form each into a ball. Transfer to the baking tray and flatten. Cover with a tea towel and leave to rise for 15 minutes. Preheat the oven to 220°C (425°F/Gas 7).

6  Lightly dust the dough with flour, then cut a 5mm (¼in) deep square in the top of each. Bake for 10 minutes, reduce the temperature to 190°C (375°F/Gas 5), and bake for a further 25–35 minutes, or until the bases sound hollow when tapped. Transfer to a wire rack and leave to cool.

**makes 2 loaves**

**prep 20 mins,
plus rising
• cook 35–45 mins**

**freeze for up to
3 months**

# Plaited loaf

This enriched fruit loaf makes a lovely teatime treat, and it's also great toasted.

## INGREDIENTS

250ml (8fl oz) whipping cream
500g (1lb 2oz) plain flour
7g sachet fast-action dried yeast
85g (3 oz) caster sugar
few drops of pure vanilla extract
zest of 1 lemon

pinch of salt
3 eggs
oil, for greasing
flour, for dusting
200g (7 oz) raisins
2 tsp milk

## METHOD

1 To make the dough, gently warm the cream in a small saucepan. Mix together the flour and dried yeast in a large bowl, then add the sugar, vanilla extract, lemon zest, and salt.

2 Separate 1 of the eggs and set aside the yolk. Add the egg white to the flour mixture, along with the remaining 2 eggs and the warmed cream. Using a wooden spoon or mixer with a kneading hook, start mixing gently to combine the ingredients, then mix and knead together for about 5 minutes, or until it forms a smooth dough. Cover with a tea towel and put in a warm place until doubled in size.

3 Grease a large baking tray. Dust the dough with flour and add the raisins. Remove from the bowl and knead briefly on a lightly floured surface until everything is incorporated. Take two-thirds of the dough and make 3 x 40cm (16in) long sausage shapes. Plait them together and put onto the baking tray. Using a rolling pin, make a depression lengthways along the whole plaited bun.

4 Beat together the reserved egg yolk and milk and brush the depression with a little of this mixture. Divide the remaining dough into 3 equal portions, roll into thin sausage shapes about 35cm (14in) long and plait. Place this plait into the depression on the larger plait and brush all over with the egg and milk. Return, uncovered, to a warm place until it has doubled in size.

5 Preheat the oven to 180°C (350°F/Gas 4). Bake loaf for 40 minutes, or until golden brown and well risen. Leave to cool on a wire rack before serving.

**makes 1 loaf**

**prep 35 mins,
plus rising
• cook 40 mins**

# Brioche

## A sweet morning bread that is ideally served warm.

### INGREDIENTS
375g (13 oz) strong white flour
50g (1¾ oz) caster sugar
7g sachet fast-action dried yeast
2 tsp salt
100ml (3½fl oz) milk, warmed
4 eggs, 1 beaten for glazing
175g (6 oz) unsalted butter, softened
oil, for greasing

### METHOD
1 Mix together the flour, sugar, yeast, and salt, then add the milk and 3 of the eggs. Mix to a dough and knead for 10 minutes. Add the butter and knead for another 10 minutes. Put the dough in a lightly oiled bowl and refrigerate overnight. (To mix using an electric mixer, see step-by-step technique on p5.)
2 Grease the tins. Lightly knead the dough, then divide into 12 pieces. Cut a quarter off 1 piece, and form both pieces into balls. Place the large ball in the tin and the small ball of dough on top, securing it by pressing the floured handle of a wooden spoon through the centre. Repeat with the remaining dough.
3 Cover loosely and leave to rise for 30 minutes. Preheat the oven to 190°C (375°F/Gas 5). Glaze the risen brioche with the beaten egg, making sure it doesn't drip down the sides. Bake for 10–12 minutes, or until golden brown, and cool on a wire rack.

makes 12
brioche

prep 35–45 mins, plus
chilling and rising
• cook 10–12 mins

chill the
dough overnight

12 × 7.5cm (3in)
brioche tins

# Crusty white loaf

A basic white bread dough that you can use
for various shapes of loaf, or rolls.

## INGREDIENTS

450g (1lb) strong plain flour, plus extra
  for dusting
1½ tsp fast-action dried yeast
1 tsp salt
1 tsp sugar
1 tbsp vegetable oil, sunflower, or
  light olive oil, plus extra for oiling

## METHOD

1 Stir the flour and yeast together in a large bowl, then mix in the salt and sugar. Make a well in the middle and pour in the oil and 300ml (10fl oz) tepid water. Mix to form a soft dough, adding more water if required.

2 Turn out on to a lightly floured work surface and knead the dough for 5–10 minutes, or until smooth and elastic. Shape into a round by tucking all of the edges into the middle, then put into a large oiled bowl, smooth-side up. Cover loosely with oiled cling film and leave in a warm place for 1 hour, or until doubled in size.

3 Oil and flour the inside of the loaf tin, tapping out the excess flour. When the dough has risen, lightly knead the dough and press it into a rough rectangle shape. Tuck the shorter ends in, followed by the longer edges, then lay it, seam-side down, in the loaf tin. Cover loosely with the oiled cling film and leave for 30 minutes, or until risen.

4 Preheat the oven to 220°C (425°F/Gas 7). Dust the top of the loaf with more flour, slash the top with a sharp knife, then bake for 20 minutes. Reduce the oven to 200°C (400°F/ Gas 6) and bake for another 20 minutes, or until risen with a golden crust. Turn out the loaf and check that it is cooked; it will sound hollow when tapped on the base. Transfer to a wire rack to cool.

makes 1
large loaf

prep 35 mins,
plus rising
• cook 40 mins

900g (2lb)
loaf tin

freeze for up to
1 month

# Crumpets

Toasted crumpets are great with sweet or savoury toppings.

## INGREDIENTS

125g (4½ oz) plain white flour
125g (4½ oz) strong white flour
½ tsp fast-action dried yeast
175ml (6fl oz) tepid milk
½ tsp salt
½ tsp bicarbonate of soda

## METHOD

1 Mix together the flours and yeast. Stir in the milk and 175ml (6fl oz) tepid water, and leave for 2 hours, or until the bubbles have risen and then started to fall again. Mix the salt and bicarbonate of soda into 2 tablespoons of lukewarm water and whisk into the batter. Set aside for 5 minutes.

2 Oil 4 crumpet rings. Lightly oil a large, heavy frying pan and place the rings in the pan.

3 Pour the batter into a jug. Heat the pan over a medium heat and pour batter into each ring to a depth of 1–2cm (½–¾in). Cook the crumpets for 8–10 minutes, or until the batter has set all the way through and the top is covered in holes. If no bubbles appear, the mixture is too dry so stir a little water into the remaining batter.

4 Lift the rings off the crumpets, turn them over, and cook for another 2–3 minutes, or until just golden. Repeat with the remaining batter. Serve the freshly cooked crumpets warm and buttered, or toast to reheat if serving them later.

**makes 8**

**prep 10 mins, plus resting • cook 20–26 mins**

**crumpet rings or 10cm (4in) metal cutters**

**freeze for up to 1 month**

# Ciabatta

This slipper-shaped Italian bread is made using a starter that rises overnight.

## INGREDIENTS

450g (1lb) Italian "oo" flour
1½ tsp fast-action dried yeast
2 tsp olive oil, plus extra for brushing
1 tsp salt

### For the starter

175g (6 oz) Italian "oo" flour
¼ tsp fast-action dried yeast

## METHOD

1 To make the starter, place the flour, yeast, and 100ml (3½fl oz) lukewarm water in a bowl. Mix well for a few minutes until the mixture forms a ball. Place inside a lightly oiled bowl, roll around the bowl to coat in the oil, cover, and leave overnight in a warm place.

2 The next day, make the dough by mixing the flour, yeast, oil, salt, and 350ml (12fl oz) tepid water. Once combined, add the starter and continue kneading until you have a wet, sticky dough.

3 Place the dough in a lightly oiled bowl. Roll it around the bowl to coat in the oil, then leave to rise in a warm place for 2 hours, or until doubled in size.

4 Preheat the oven to 220°C (425°F/Gas 7). Punch the dough back and knead for 10 minutes, or until smooth and elastic. Mould the dough into a slipper shape and place it on an oiled baking tray. Bake for 10 minutes, reduce the temperature to 190°C (375°F/Gas 5), and bake for a further 30 minutes, or until a crust forms and the loaf sounds hollow when tapped underneath. Cool on a wire rack.

makes 1 loaf

prep 30 mins, plus standing and rising • cook 40 mins

make the starter the day before baking

# Onion and herb loaf

A delicious savoury loaf with herb-flavoured dough and a fried onion filling.

## INGREDIENTS

550g (1¼lb) strong white flour
1 tsp fast-action dried yeast
1 heaped tsp salt
1 tbsp finely chopped rosemary, plus
  2–3 extra sprigs, rubbed in oil
5 tbsp extra virgin olive oil
1 egg, beaten

### For the filling

2 tbsp olive oil
½ tsp salt
½ tsp coarsely crushed black pepper
2 onions, sliced
1 tbsp balsamic vinegar
3 tbsp golden caster sugar
1 tbsp rosemary or thyme, finely chopped

## METHOD

1 Place 225g (8 oz) of the flour in a bowl, add 300ml (10fl oz) tepid water and the yeast, mix well, and leave for 1 hour. Add the remaining flour, salt, rosemary, and oil, and mix to a soft, pliable dough. Knead on a lightly floured surface for 10 minutes, or until elastic.

2 Shape the dough into a ball and place in a large oiled bowl. Cover loosely with oiled cling film, and leave in a warm place for 1 hour, or until doubled in size.

3 For the filling, heat the oil in a frying pan, add the salt and black pepper, then add the onions and fry on a medium heat for 10 minutes, or until golden. Stir in the remaining ingredients and fry for 2–4 minutes, or until dark and sticky.

4 Turn the dough out on to a floured surface and knead briefly. Press into a large rectangle shape, then spread with the filling. Fold the shorter sides in, then fold the bottom third up, and the top third down, like an envelope. Press gently, then turn over and lift onto a lightly floured baking tray, and shape the ends of the loaf into slight points. Cover loosely and leave for 30 minutes, or until doubled in size. Preheat the oven to 220°C (425°F/Gas 7).

5 Brush the dough with beaten egg, sprinkle with flour, then slash it with a sharp knife to reveal the filling inside. Sprinkle with the rosemary rubbed in oil, then bake for 20 minutes. Reduce the oven to 200°C (400°F/Gas 6) and bake for 20 minutes, or until the bread is risen and a deep golden brown.

makes 1 loaf

prep 35 mins, plus
rising • cook 55 mins

# English muffins

A soft traditional English bread that is great for brunch.

## INGREDIENTS

450g (1lb) strong white flour
1 tsp fast-action dried yeast
1 tsp salt
25g (scant 1 oz) butter, melted
25g (scant 1 oz) ground rice or semolina

## METHOD

1 Mix the flour, yeast, and salt in a large bowl. Add the melted butter and 300ml (10fl oz) tepid water and mix to a soft, pliable dough.

2 Knead the dough for 5 minutes. Shape into a ball and place in a large oiled bowl. Cover loosely with oiled cling film and leave in a warm place for 1 hour, or until doubled in size. Lay a tea towel on a tray and scatter with most of the ground rice.

3 Turn out the dough, knead briefly, and divide into 10 balls. Place on the tea towel and press into flattish rounds. Sprinkle with the rest of the ground rice and cover with another tea towel. Leave for 20–30 minutes, or until risen.

4 Heat a large lidded frying pan and cook the muffins in batches. Cover with the lid and cook very gently for 10–12 minutes, or until they puff up and the undersides are golden and toasted. Turn over and cook for 3–4 minutes, or until golden underneath. Cool on a wire rack.

makes 10

prep 25–30 mins, plus
rising • cook 13–16 mins

# Spiced fruit buns

These delicious sweetened rolls make a perfect afternoon snack.

## INGREDIENTS

500g (1lb 2oz) strong white bread flour
7g sachet fast-action dried yeast
1 tsp mixed spice
½ tsp ground nutmeg
1 tsp salt
6 tbsp caster sugar

60g (2 oz) butter
240ml (8fl oz) tepid milk
150g (5½ oz) mixed dried fruit
2 tbsp icing sugar
¼ tsp pure vanilla extract

## METHOD

1 Place the flour, yeast, spices, salt, and caster sugar in a large mixing bowl. Rub in the butter. Add enough milk to form a soft, pliable dough. Knead well for 10 minutes. Shape into a ball, then place in a lightly oiled bowl and cover loosely. Leave in a warm place to rise for 1 hour.

2 Tip the dough on to a lightly floured work surface and knead gently. Knead in the dried fruit. Divide the dough into 12 pieces, roll into balls, and place, well spaced, on lightly greased baking trays. Cover loosely and place in a warm place for 30 minutes, or until doubled in size.

3 Preheat the oven to 200°C (400°F/Gas 6). Bake for 15 minutes, or until the buns sound hollow when tapped on the bottom. Transfer to a wire rack to cool. While the buns are still hot, combine the icing sugar, vanilla extract, and 1 tbsp cold water, and brush over the top of the buns to glaze.

makes 12

prep 30 mins, plus
rising • cook 15 mins

# Rye bread

Breads made with rye flour are very popular in central and eastern Europe.

## INGREDIENTS

150g (5½ oz) rye flour

200g (7 oz) strong white flour, plus extra for dusting

2 tsp salt

1 egg, beaten

1 tsp caraway seeds, to decorate

### For the starter

150g (5½ oz) rye flour

150g (5½ oz) pot live natural yogurt

1 tsp fast-action dried yeast

1 tbsp black treacle

1 tsp caraway seeds, lightly crushed

## METHOD

1 Mix all of the starter ingredients together with 250ml (9fl oz) tepid water. Cover and leave overnight, until bubbling.

2 The next day, mix the flours together with the salt, then stir into the starter. Mix to make a dough, adding a little extra water if required.

3 Turn out on to a lightly floured surface and knead the dough for 5–10 minutes, or until smooth and springy. Shape into a ball, put into an oiled bowl and cover loosely with oiled cling film. Leave in a warm place for 1 hour, or until doubled in size.

4 Flour a baking tray. Lightly knead the dough again, then form it into a rugby-ball shape. Lift on to the tray, re-cover it loosely, and leave to rise again for another 30 minutes. Preheat the oven to 220°C (425°F/Gas 7).

5 Brush the dough with the egg, sprinkle with the caraway seeds, and slash the loaf along its length with a sharp knife. Bake for 20 minutes, then reduce the heat to 200°C (400°F/Gas 6) and bake for another 20–30 minutes, or until dark golden with a hard shiny crust. Cool on a wire rack.

makes 1
large loaf

prep 25 mins,
plus rising
• cook 40–50 mins

make the
starter the day
before baking

# Scotch pancakes

These thick, little pancakes are also called drop scones because the batter is dropped onto a frying pan.

## INGREDIENTS
225g (8 oz) plain white flour
4 tsp baking powder
1 large egg
2 tsp golden syrup
200ml (7fl oz) milk
vegetable oil, for frying

## METHOD
1 Place the frying pan over a medium heat. Fold a tea towel in half and lay it on a baking tray.
2 Sift the flour and baking powder into a bowl; make a well in the centre and add the egg, golden syrup, and milk. Whisk well to make a smooth batter the consistency of thick cream. If the mixture is too thick, beat in a little more milk.
3 Test that the frying pan is hot enough by sprinkling a little flour on to the hot surface; it should slowly brown. If it burns, the pan is too hot and needs to cool a little. When the temperature is right, carefully dust off the flour and rub a piece of kitchen towel dipped in cooking oil lightly over the surface. Use oven gloves to protect your hands.
4 Lift out 1 tablespoon of batter, cleaning the back of the spoon on the edge of the bowl. Drop the batter from the tip of the spoon on to the hot pan to make a nice round shape. Repeat, leaving enough room between the rounds for the pancakes to rise and spread.
5 Bubbles will appear on the surface of the pancakes. When they begin to burst, ease a palette knife underneath the pancakes and gently flip to cook the other side. To ensure even browning, lightly press the flat blade on the cooked side after you have turned the pancake; place cooked pancakes inside the folded towel to keep them soft while you fry the rest of the batch.
6 Oil the hot pan after each batch and watch the heat. If the pancakes are pale and take a long time to cook, turn up the heat. If they brown too quickly on the outside and are still raw in the middle, reduce the heat. They are best eaten freshly baked and warm.

makes 12

prep 10 mins
• cook 15 mins

freeze for up to
1 month

# Scones

**There is nothing better for afternoon tea than freshly baked crumbly scones.**

## INGREDIENTS

225g (8 oz) self-raising flour, plus extra
   for dusting
½ tsp salt
50g (1¾ oz) sultanas
60g (2 oz) butter, cubed
30g (1 oz) sugar
150ml (5fl oz) milk
1 egg, beaten

## METHOD

1  Preheat the oven to 220°C (425°F/Gas 7). Sift the flour and the salt into a large mixing bowl, then add the sultanas and mix together. Rub in the butter with your fingertips, until the mixture resembles coarse breadcrumbs, then mix in the sugar. Make a well in the centre and pour in the milk, then stir together, bringing in the flour from the edges, with a knife or spoon.
2  Turn the soft, sticky dough on to a lightly floured work surface. Knead until smooth, then shape into a 2.5cm (1in) thick circle.
3  Dip the cutter in flour, then use to cut rounds from the dough. Re-form the dough, if necessary, to cut sufficient scones.
4  Place the scones on a baking tray and brush the tops with a little beaten egg. Put the tray on to the top shelf of the oven and bake for 12–15 minutes, or until golden. Remove from the oven and cool on a wire rack. Serve while still warm.

**makes 8**

**prep 25 mins**
**• cook 12–15 mins**

**6cm (2½in) round
pastry cutter**

# Mini chocolate nut pastries

Tasty bite-sized chocolate pastries – the perfect treat.

## INGREDIENTS
115g (4 oz) ground hazelnuts
1½ tbsp icing sugar, plus extra
   for dusting
3 tbsp amaretto or almond-flavoured
   liqueur
75g (2½ oz) dark chocolate, grated
4 x filo pastry sheets, 18 x 30cm
   (7 x 12in)
3 tbsp clear honey, warmed

## METHOD
1 Preheat the oven to 190°C (375°F/Gas 5). Lightly grease a baking tray. Mix the
   hazelnuts, icing sugar, amaretto, and chocolate until combined.
2 Cut out 24 squares, each 10cm (4in), from the filo. Place some filling in the middle of
   each square. Brush a little water around the edge, gather the sides around the filling,
   and pinch into a purse-like shape.
3 Place the pastries on the baking tray and bake for 10–12 minutes, or until golden. Brush
   gently with honey, leave for 5 minutes, then dust with icing sugar. Serve warm or cold.

makes 24

prep 25 mins
• cook 10–12 mins

# Blueberry cream cheese tart

Juicy blueberries perfectly complement the creamy filling.

## INGREDIENTS

115g (4 oz) cream cheese
60g (2 oz) soured cream
60g (2 oz) caster sugar
pinch of grated nutmeg
3 eggs, beaten
zest of 1 lemon
350g (12 oz) blueberries
icing sugar, to serve

### For the pastry

175g (6 oz) plain flour
85g (3 oz) butter, diced
2 tbsp caster sugar
1 egg yolk

## METHOD

1 Place the flour, butter, and sugar in a food processor, and pulse until it resembles breadcrumbs. Or, rub the butter into the flour with your fingertips until it resembles breadcrumbs, then stir in the sugar.

2 Add the egg yolk and mix to a firm dough. Roll out the pastry on a lightly floured surface and use to line the flan tin. Prick the base with a fork. Chill for at least 30 minutes. Preheat the oven to 200°C (400°F/Gas 6).

3 Line the pastry case with greaseproof paper and fill with baking beans. Bake for 10 minutes, then remove the paper and beans and bake for another 10 minutes, or until pale golden. Remove from the oven and reduce the temperature to 180°C (350°F/Gas 4).

4 Beat together the cream cheese, soured cream, sugar, nutmeg, eggs, and lemon zest until well combined. Pour into the pastry case and scatter the blueberries over the surface. Bake for 25–30 minutes, or until just set. Allow to cool before transferring to a serving plate. Serve warm or cold, dusted with icing sugar.

serves 8       prep 25 mins,        23cm (9in) loose-
               plus chilling •       bottomed flan tin
               cook 45–60 mins       • baking beans

# Key lime pie

This pie is named for the small limes that grow in the Florida Keys.

## INGREDIENTS

100g (3½ oz) butter
225g (8 oz) digestive biscuits, crushed

### For the filling

5 limes, plus 1 extra, cut into thin
    slices, to decorate
3 large egg yolks
400g can condensed milk

## METHOD

1 Preheat the oven to 180°C (350°F/Gas 4). Melt the butter in a saucepan over a low heat. Add the digestive biscuit crumbs and stir until well combined. Remove from the heat and tip the mixture into the flan tin, then use the base of a metal spoon to press it evenly and firmly all over the base and sides of the tin. Place on a baking tray and bake for 5–10 minutes.

2 Meanwhile, grate the zest of 3 of the limes into a bowl. Juice all 5 of the limes, and set aside.

3 Place the egg yolks into the bowl with the lime zest, and whisk until the egg has thickened. Pour in the condensed milk and continue whisking for 5 minutes if using an electric whisk, or for 6–7 minutes if whisking by hand. Add the lime juice, and whisk again until it is incorporated. Pour the mixture into the tin and bake for 15–20 minutes, or until it is set.

4 Remove the pie from the oven and leave it to cool completely. Serve the pie decorated with the lime slices.

**serves 8**

**prep 20–25 mins plus cooling • cook 15–20 mins**

**23cm (9in) loose-bottomed flan tin**

# Lemon tart

Variations of this ever-popular tart often appear on restaurant menus.

## INGREDIENTS

5 eggs
200g (7 oz) caster sugar
zest and juice of 4 lemons
250ml (9fl oz) double cream
icing sugar, to serve
lemon zest, to serve

### For the pastry

175g (6 oz) plain flour, plus
  extra for dusting
85g (3 oz) butter, chilled
45g (1½ oz) caster sugar
1 egg

## METHOD

1 To make the pastry, place the flour, butter, and sugar into a food processor and pulse until it resembles breadcrumbs. Add the egg and process until the pastry draws together into a ball.

2 Roll out the pastry on a lightly floured surface into a large circle to line the tart tin. Chill for at least 30 minutes.

3 Beat the eggs and sugar together until combined. Beat in the lemon zest and juice, then whisk in the cream. Chill for 1 hour.

4 Preheat the oven to 190°C (375°F/Gas 5). Line the pastry case with greaseproof paper, fill with baking beans, and bake blind for 10 minutes. Remove the paper and beans, and bake for 5 minutes, or until the base is crisp.

5 Reduce the oven to 140°C (275°F/Gas 1). Place the tart tin on a baking tray. Pour in the lemon filling, being careful not to allow the filling to spill over the edges. Bake for 30 minutes, or until just set. Remove from the oven and cool. Serve, dusted with icing sugar and sprinkled with lemon zest over the top.

serves 8

prep 35 mins, plus
chilling and cooling •
cook 45 mins

food processor • 24cm
(9in) loose-bottomed
tart tin • baking beans

# Cannoli

Indulge in crisp Sicilian pastries filled with glacé fruits and ricotta cheese.

## INGREDIENTS

175g (6 oz) plain flour, plus extra
   for rolling and dusting
pinch of salt
60g (2 oz) butter
45g (1½ oz) caster sugar
1 egg, beaten
2–3 tbsp dry white wine or Marsala
1 egg white, lightly beaten
oil, for deep-frying

### For the filling

60g (2 oz) dark chocolate,
   grated or very finely chopped
350g (12 oz) ricotta cheese
60g (2 oz) icing sugar, plus
   extra to dust
finely grated zest of 1 orange
60g (2 oz) chopped glacé fruits
   or candied citrus peel

## METHOD

1 To make the pastry, sift the flour and salt into a bowl, and rub in the butter. Stir in the sugar, mix in the beaten egg, and add enough wine to make a soft dough. Knead until smooth.

2 Roll out the pastry thinly and cut into 16 squares, each measuring roughly 7.5cm (3in). Dust 4 cannoli moulds with flour and wrap a pastry square loosely around each on the diagonal, dampening the edges with lightly beaten egg white and pressing them together to seal.

3 Heat the oil for deep-frying to 180°C (350°F) and deep-fry for 3–4 minutes, or until the pastry is golden and crisp. Drain on a plate lined with kitchen paper, and, when cool enough to handle, carefully twist the metal tubes so you can pull them out of the pastry. Cook 3 more batches in the same way.

4 To make the filling, mix together all the ingredients. When the pastry tubes are cold, pipe or spoon the filling into them. Dust with icing sugar to serve.

**makes 16**

**prep 30 mins,
plus cooling •
cook 20 mins**

**deep-fat fryer or large
saucepan half filled with
oil • cannoli moulds**

**freeze the uncooked
pastry for up to
3 months**

# Pear and cinnamon strudel

Hailing from Austria, strudels encase fruit fillings in layers of flaky pastry.

## INGREDIENTS
4 ripe pears, peeled and sliced
2 tsp ground cinnamon
handful of raisins
1–2 tbsp golden caster sugar
15 sheets filo pastry
knob of butter, melted, to brush

## METHOD
1 Preheat the oven to 200°C (400°F/Gas 6). Line a baking sheet with baking parchment. Place the pear, cinnamon, raisins, and sugar in a bowl, mix well, then put to one side. Brushing the sheets of filo with a little melted butter as you go, layer 3 sheets on the baking sheet, then layer another 3 next to them.
2 Sit another 3 layers of filo pastry on top, placing them with the long edges facing in the other direction. Repeat with another layer of 3 so you have an oblong-shaped base. Spoon the filling down the centre, then fold over the edges. Top with a final layer of 3 sheets of filo and brush the whole thing with butter. Bake in the oven for 30–40 minutes, or until golden brown.

serves 4

prep time 10 mins
• cook time 40 mins

# Florentines

These crisp Italian biscuits are packed full of fruit and nuts, and coated with a thin layer of luxurious dark chocolate.

## INGREDIENTS

60g (2 oz) butter
60g (2 oz) caster sugar
1 tbsp clear honey
60g (2 oz) plain flour
45g (1½ oz) chopped mixed peel
45g (1½ oz) glacé cherries, finely
  chopped
45g (1½ oz) blanched almonds,
  finely chopped
1 tsp lemon juice
1 tbsp double cream
175g (6 oz) dark chocolate

## METHOD

1 Preheat the oven to 180°C (350°F/Gas 4) and line 2 baking trays with greaseproof paper.
2 Put the butter, sugar, and honey into a small saucepan, and melt gently over a low heat. Then allow to cool until it is just warm. Stir in the next 6 ingredients.
3 Drop teaspoonfuls of the mixture on to the baking trays, leaving space between them for the biscuits to spread.
4 Bake for 10 minutes, or until golden. Do not let them get too dark. Leave them on the baking tray for a few minutes, before lifting them on to a wire rack to cool completely.
5 Break the chocolate into pieces, and put it into a heatproof bowl set over a pan of gently simmering water. Make sure the bowl is not touching the water. Once the chocolate has melted, spread a thin layer of chocolate on the bottom of each biscuit, and place, chocolate-side up, on the wire rack to set. Spread a second layer of chocolate over the first layer. Just before the chocolate sets, make wavy lines in it with a fork.

makes 16–20

prep 20 mins
• cook 15–20 mins

# Rich chocolate biscuits

Use good-quality chocolate and cocoa powder to make these biscuits really tasty.

## INGREDIENTS
100g (3½ oz) butter, softened
50g (1¾ oz) caster sugar
125g (4½ oz) plain flour
25g (scant 1 oz) cocoa powder
melted dark chocolate or milk
  chocolate, to drizzle (optional)

## METHOD
1 Preheat the oven to 180°C (350°F/Gas 4). Line 2 baking trays with baking parchment. In a bowl, mix the butter and sugar together with an electric hand whisk or mixer until pale and creamy. Sift in the flour and cocoa powder, and beat until the mixture comes together to form a dough. You may need to bring it together with your hands at the end.
2 Roll the dough into 16 walnut-sized balls and place them on the baking trays. Press the middle of each one with your thumb to flatten it, or use a fork, which will decorate it at the same time. Bake for 20 minutes, then transfer to a wire rack to cool completely. Drizzle over the melted chocolate (if using), and allow to set before serving.

**makes 16**

**prep 15 mins, plus cooling • cook 20 mins**

**electric hand whisk or mixer**

London, New York, Melbourne, Munich, and Delhi

Senior Editor Cécile Landau

Editorial Assistant Shashwati Tia Sarkar

Designer Elma Aquino

Jacket Designer Mark Penfound

DTP Designer Kavita Varma

## DK INDIA

Editorial Consultant Dipali Singh

Designer Neha Ahuja

DTP Designer Tarun Sharma

DTP Coordinator Sunil Sharma

Head of Publishing Aparna Sharma

This edition published in 2013
First published in Great Britain in 2012.
Material in this publication was previously published
in *The Cooking Book* (2008) and *Cook Express* (2009)
by Dorling Kindersley Limited
80 Strand, London WC2R 0RL
Penguin Group (UK)

10 9 8 7 6 5 4 3 2 1
001-192527-Feb/13

A CIP catalogue record for this book is available
from the British Library.

ISBN 978-1-4093-2592-5

Printed and bound in China by Hung Hing Printing Co. Ltd.